Make your own Gifts

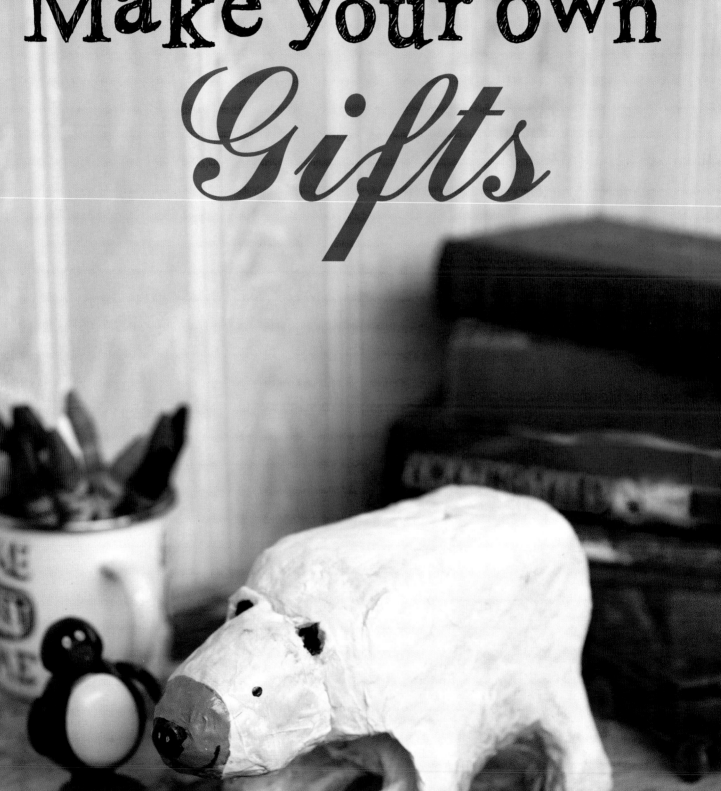

LONDON, NEW YORK, MUNICH,
MELBOURNE, and DELHI

Senior designer Sonia Moore
Senior editor Carrie Love
Design Poppy Joslin, Ria Holland,
and Sadie Thomas
Jacket designer Rosie Levine
Additional editing Jennifer Lane,
Katy Lennon, James Mitchem,
and Christine Stroyan
Photographer Will Heap
Additional photography Andy Crawford
Photo on rocket Big Smile Photography
Illustrator Bryony Fripp
Home economist Annie Nichols
Crafters Lucy Barnfather, June Hall,
Ria Holland, Sonia Moore,
Chris Stewart, and Rose Thunberg
Models Lara Duffy, Charlotte Johnson,
Scarlett Joslin, and Max Moore
Production editor Sarah Isle
Production controller Ché Creasey
Creative director Jane Bull
Category publisher Mary Ling

First published in Great Britain in 2013 by
Dorling Kindersley Limited
80 Strand, London WC2R 0RL
Penguin Group (UK)

**This edition produced for The Book People Ltd,
Hall Wood Avenue, Haydock, St Helen's
WA11 9UL**

Copyright © 2013 Dorling Kindersley Limited
A Penguin Company
10 9 8 7 6 5 4 3 2 1
001–187174–09/13

A CIP catalogue record for this book
is available from the British Library.

ISBN: 978-1-40933-891-8

Printed and bound in China
by Hung Hing

**Discover more at
www.dk.com**

Contents

Introduction

This book is loaded with brilliant crafty projects that you can make as presents for birthdays, Valentine's Day, Christmas, Mother's Day, Father's Day, and any other day that you want to give a gift! Just follow the simple photo steps and instructions, and get making!

Tag it!
Make your mark on a present by creating your own gift tag (see page 75). It's the perfect way to write someone a special message.

⚠️ Safety

All the projects in this book are to be made under adult supervision. When you see the warning triangle (above) take extra care as hot cookers and sharp implements are used to make a project. Ask an adult to help you. Always follow the packet instructions when choosing and using paint, ink, and glue.

Getting started

1 Read the instructions all the way through before you start.
2 Gather together everything you need so it's in one place.
3 Wash your hands after you use glue, ink, or paint. Don't let glue dry on your skin.
4 Protect work surfaces – lay down a plastic tablecloth or newspaper when you use paint, ink, or glue.
5 Have a cloth handy to mop up any spillages.
6 Put an apron on and tie back your hair.
7 Keep your working area well ventilated, especially when you work with paint or glue.
8 Take extra care when using a needle and thread, paper fasteners, and brooch pins.

Food wise

• When you're in the kitchen you should ask an adult to take things in and out of the oven, and to use the hob.
• Wash your hands before and after you work with food. Always wash your hands after handling raw eggs.
• Check the use-by date on all ingredients.
• The recipe projects are meant as special treats as part of a balanced diet. They're quite high in sugar so DON'T be greedy and eat too many! One portion is plenty for a child or an adult.
• Carefully weigh out the ingredients before you start a recipe or project. Use measuring spoons, weighing scales, and a measuring jug as necessary. Below are the full names and abbreviations:

Imperial measures
oz = ounce
lb = pound
fl oz = fluid ounce

Metric measures
g = gram
ml = millilitre

Spoon measures
tsp = teaspoon
tbsp = tablespoon

Paper craft
projects

Super FUN!

Rocket pen pot

5..4..3..2..1.. blast off! Surprise someone with this colourful and unique pen pot. Create a secret compartment at the back of the rocket to store smaller items for any future space missions.

Fill it with colourful pens or pencils.

I'm going to the Moon!

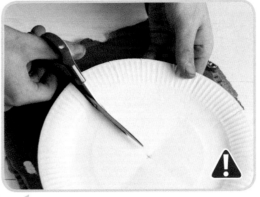

cardboard

paper plate

stapler

large paper scissors pen cardboard tube with a plastic lid

1 plastic lid from a juice carton

strong glue 2 plastic lids from milk bottles

newspaper

PVA glue acrylic paints

paintbrushes

paper cup with a lid (that will fit inside the cardboard tube)

paper fasteners

string

1 To make the rocket wings, take strong cardboard and draw 2 wing shapes (around half the height of your tube), including tabs for sticking them on. Cut the wings out and attach them to the cardboard tube using strong glue.

2 Cut a line from the edge of a paper plate into the centre. Fold the plate round into a cone shape to fit the size of the tube and staple the edges closed.

3 Attach the cone to the top of the plastic lid on the cardboard tube with strong glue.

4 Attach the 3 plastic lids flat-side down to make the portholes, with the small lid in the middle. Cover the tube and portholes with a layer of papier-mâché (see step 2 on page 21).

Add paper fasteners and a loop of string for the door handle.

5 Decorate your rocket using acrylic paints. Use light blue for the main body of the rocket, red and silver for the cone, and yellow and red for the bottom of the wings.

6 To make your secret compartment, ask an adult to cut a door at the back of the rocket. Next, ask them to cut a section from the lower side of the paper cup to match the rocket door. Drop the paper cup and lid into the tube. The lid stops pencils from falling into the secret compartment.

You will need

paper plate

scissors

cereal box, flattened

patterned wrapping paper

glue stick and strong glue

foil takeaway container with a flat base

large needle and thick thread

paper fastener

Tie a knot in the thread after you have pulled it through the bird (step 5), to hold the bird in place.

HAPPY BIRTHDAY

Birdcage

This beautiful and delicate birdcage can be given as a surprise gift to cheer someone up. It's so calming and sweet that the recipient will be instantly charmed.

TOP TIP
Make a set of cages and hang them in front of a window or as decorations for a party.

1 Take a paper plate and make small cuts all around the edge. Push the sides up so they overlap slightly and create an edge. Use the needle to make a hole in the centre of the plate.

2 Cover both sides of a flattened cereal box with patterned wrapping paper using a glue stick. Cut 5 long, thin strips about 1cm (½in) wide. Fold each strip in half to find the centre and make a hole there with the needle.

3 Cut 2 strips of card that are 3cm (1¼in) wide. Attach the wide strips of the covered card to the outside edge of the plate using strong glue, so that they encircle the plate.

Be careful of sharp edges.

4 Draw a bird shape (see template on page 76) onto a metal foil takeaway container. Cut out the shape. Draw detail onto the bird using a biro. Make a small hole on the bird's back.

5 With the needle, draw thread through the hole in the long strips. Then take the thread through the hole in the bird's back and finally through the bottom of the plate. Secure with tape.

6 Push a paper fastener through the holes in the strips so that they fan out in a star shape. Fix the end of each thin strip to the inside of the plate with strong glue. Add a message plaque.

The art of folding paper to make it into a 3-D object is called "origami". These flowers are made using this technique.

The Japanese word for these paper flowers is *Kusudama*.

Use a glitter pen to add a bit of extra sparkle to your flowers.

Flower power

These beautiful, colourful flowers will brighten up any room – from a bedroom to a kitchen – and are surprisingly simple to make. Once you've done the first petal, you just repeat until the flower is done.

1 Cut a square of paper and fold it in half to make a triangle. The easiest way to do this is to take a sheet of paper and fold one corner all the way across to the other side in a big triangle, then trim off the excess strip of paper.

2 With the fold at the bottom and the point at the top, fold the left point of the triangle up to the top point.

You will need

colourful paper, plain or patterned

strong glue   scissors

3 Repeat with the right point, to make a square which opens in the middle.

4 Take the top right point and fold it back, so that the inner folded edge comes back to line up with the outside edge of the square.

Repeat with the left-hand point. Turn to the next page to see how to make the next fold.

5 Now lift the flap up on the left-hand side, poke your fingers inside the cone shape to help fully bring it out. Then flatten the flap down on the left-hand side, as shown in the picture above, to make a kite shape. Repeat with the right-hand side flap.

6 Take the top triangle of each kite shape and fold it down flat, so that it is level with the long edge behind it.

Ta da! You've made the first petal for your *kusudama* flower.

7 Fold each long triangle in half on itself, along the fold that was made earlier, so that you end up with a square shape again.

8 Bring the sides of the triangles towards each other, gently curving the square to form the full petal.

Flower headband

You can use the same method with smaller squares of paper to make smaller flowers. Attach them to a headband or a badge using strong glue.

Make your own sheets of handmade paper (see pages 74–75) and create the petals using it.

Colour-coordinate your headband to the paper flowers.

9 Glue the 2 sides together and hold them firmly until the glue sets and you have a complete petal. Repeat steps 1–8 until you have 5 petals.

10 Join the petals together, one at a time, to make your flower. To do this, glue each petal to the next along the join, allowing each to dry before adding the next one.

When all 5 petals are in place, you can see the full effect.

Snip the pointed ends off to insert a twig onto each flower.

Heart cards

Everyone loves to receive a Valentine's Day card. You can make several designs and give them away as a surprise. Follow these steps to make a 3-D heart card using strips of coloured paper.

1 Cut the coloured strips to the right lengths. You will need two of each colour per card, so if you want to make a few cards do this all at once.

You will need

A4 white card

scissors

PVA glue

red paper cut into 1cm (½in) x 14cm (5½in) strips

orange paper cut into 1cm (½in) x 16cm (6¼in) strips

yellow paper cut into 1cm (½in) x 18cm (7in) strips

green paper cut into 1cm (½in) x 20½cm (8in) strips

blue paper cut into 1cm (½in) x 23cm (9in) strips

purple paper cut into 1cm (½in) x 25cm (10in) strips

Or, for a different design, cut out 8 paper hearts from different coloured paper that go up in size, starting with the smallest. Fold each heart in half and stick them down inside each other using PVA glue.

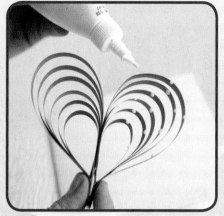

2 Starting with the smallest and working your way up, bend the strips into loops to make half a heart. Glue each loop into place as you go.

3 Repeat to make the other half, then glue them together using PVA glue. Then apply small drops of PVA glue to the back of the heart.

4 Stick the heart down in the middle of a square piece of card roughly 18cm x 18cm (7in x7in). PVA glue dries clear so don't worry if it goes everywhere.

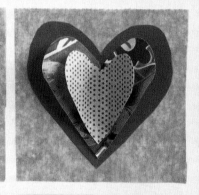

Add curls to your fairy's hair by winding the strands around a wooden skewer.

Don't forget to give your fairy hands by looping the pipe cleaner round and then leaving a little extra for a thumb.

Your fairy's hand can be bent to hold a wand.

Fairy decoration

Make someone's wish come true with this beautiful paper craft creation. You can make fairy decorations for a Christmas tree or just for fun. A fairy can bring magic into a room at any time of year.

1 Wrap a piece of A4 coloured card round into a cone shape and use a strong glue to glue the edge down. For extra hold, staple it in place.

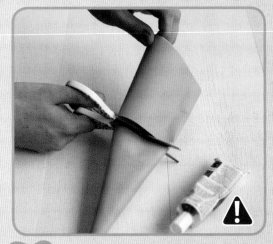

2 Cut the top end of the cone shape off, leaving the length you want your fairy's body to be. Don't forget that she will have legs too.

3 For the fairy's legs, bend one end of a pipe cleaner to make a foot. Thread beads onto the pipe cleaner, then bend the other end to make the other foot. Bend the pipe cleaner in half and glue the middle to the inside back of the body.

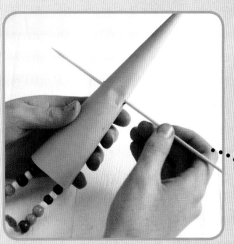

4 Using a wooden skewer, make a hole through both sides of the card. Point the skewer away from your body when doing so. Feed through a pipe cleaner to make your fairy's arms.

Twist one end
of each petal.

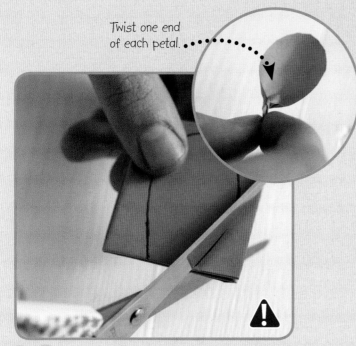

5 For the fairy's skirt, cut a sheet of A4 paper
into squares and stack them in piles of 2 or 3.
Draw a petal shape on the top piece of paper in
each pile and use sharp scissors to cut out the
petal shapes.

6 Use strong glue to stick the petals on for your fairy's
skirt. Build up two layers of the skirt around her body,
starting with the bottom layer.

Curl the end of each strand
around a wooden skewer.

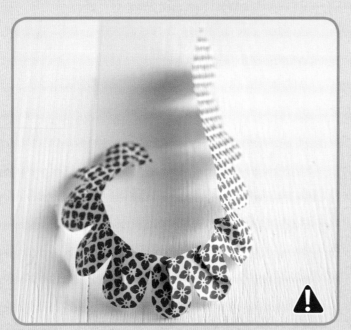

7 Make the top layer of your fairy's skirt from a piece of
patterned paper. Ask an adult to help cut the curves for
you, then glue this above the petals. If you want, make a belt
for her too, from a strip of ribbon.

8 Fold a piece of coloured paper into 4 columns.
Cut a square off the end of the folded paper
about 6cm (2¹/₂in) long. Cut a rectangular chunk
from either side of the square, then cut in about
8 lines to make the strands of your fairy's hair.

Santa

You can use the same method to make a Santa Claus to keep your fairy company. Just add a hat, a beard, and a sack of toys!

Cut Santa a rectangular face and make small cuts in one of the long ends for his beard and hair at the back. Wrap around the top of his body.

For Santa's hat, just fold over the top of the cone and add a pom-pom on the end to cover the point.

Give fairy some glittery wings for a really festive look.

9 For your fairy's face, cut a circle from a piece of pink paper. To give her rosy cheeks, use two circles from a piece of darker pink paper. Draw a nose, eyes, and a mouth in black pen. Use strong glue to fix your fairy's face to her head.

10 Fold over the pointy top of your fairy's head, make a hole and tie some string through it to suspend her. Stick on your fairy's hair, framing her face. Finally, cut a crown and sleeves and glue them on. Your fairy is dressed.

Polar bear bank

Make the heart of the person who receives this gift melt. They will cherish this beautiful papier-mâché polar bear money bank. Unlike most money banks, you don't need to break in to get to your funds, thanks to a clever screw-on polar bear head.

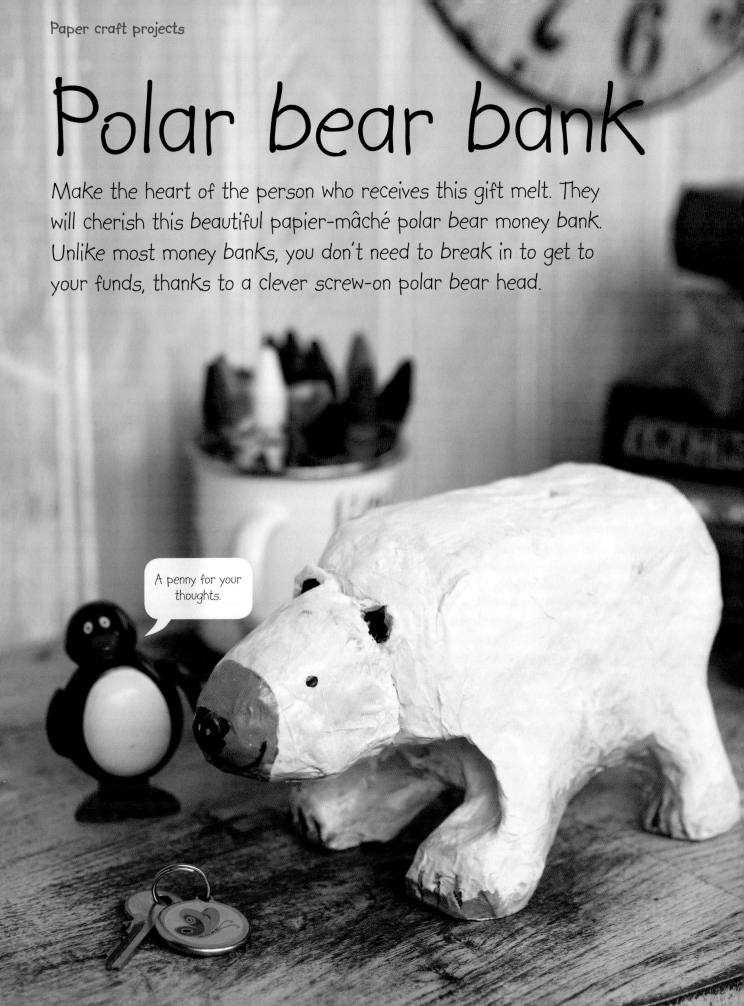

20

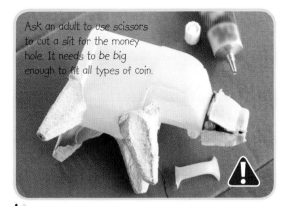

Ask an adult to use scissors to cut a slit for the money hole. It needs to be big enough to fit all types of coin.

1 Cut four dividers from an egg box to use for the polar bear's legs. Attach them to the milk bottle using strong glue. With the lid screwed onto the bottle, attach an egg box cup for the head, then unscrew and remove the head.

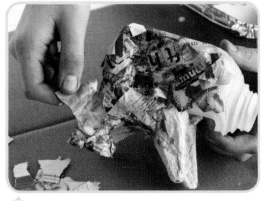

2 Use PVA glue to stick newspaper pieces all over the bear's body. This technique is called papier-mâché. Scrunch up balls of newspaper dipped in glue to build up the bear's bottom, feet, and nose (see step 3).

You will need

egg box

scissors

strong glue

PVA glue

1 pint milk bottle

newspaper

paintbrushes

black, white, and brown acrylic paint

3 Make cardboard ears (from the egg box) for your polar bear and glue them onto the top of his head. Build out the length of the nose with lots of small balls of newspaper and PVA glue. This takes time and patience.

Keep the head and body apart until the papier-mâché has dried.

4 Add a few layers of papier-mâché to strengthen the bear. Allow drying time between each layer. It usually takes at least a few hours to dry, but it's best to leave it overnight to fully dry out.

5 When the papier-mâché has dried, use acrylic paints to bring your polar bear to life.

6 Use black paint to give your bear a friendly face, and brown paint for his nose.

Open up your bottle to retrieve your coins!

Stand up card

Wish someone a happy birthday in a totally different way by giving them a 3-D card that stands up by itself. All it takes is a little cutting, glueing, and imagination!

You will need

scissors

flattened cereal box

glue stick

coloured pencils and pens

decorative paper to collage with

⚠ Colour and decorate the template however you like. Then cut the pieces out along the dotted lines and slot them together like this.

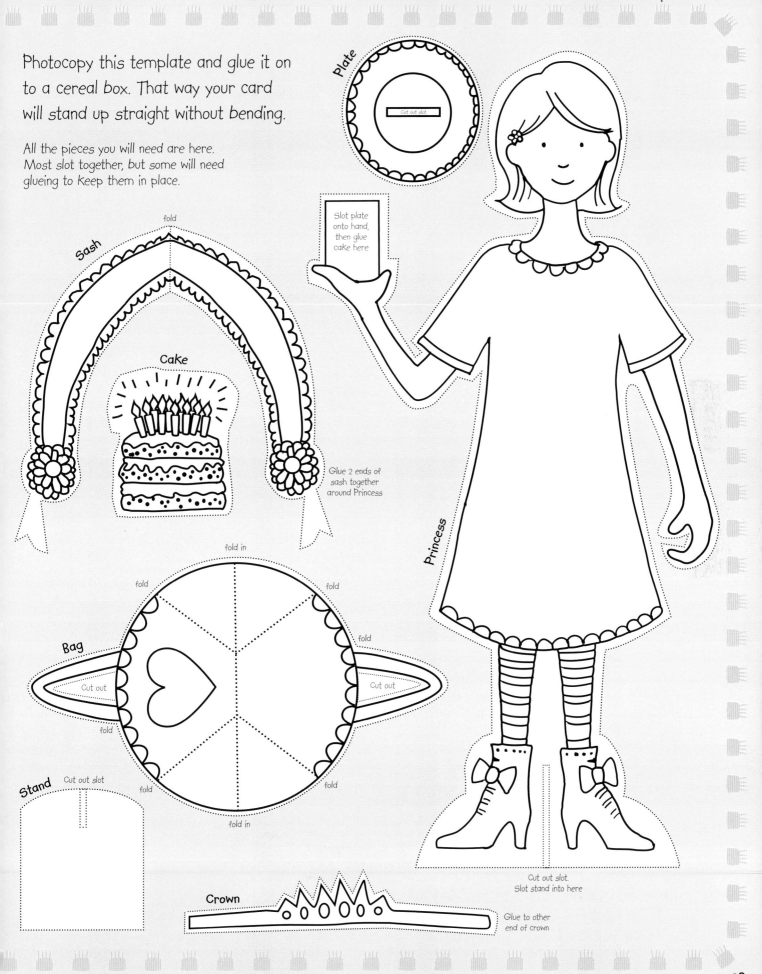

Photocopy this template and glue it on to a cereal box. That way your card will stand up straight without bending.

All the pieces you will need are here. Most slot together, but some will need glueing to keep them in place.

Plate

Cut out slot

Slot plate onto hand, then glue cake here

Sash

Cake

Glue 2 ends of sash together around Princess

fold

fold in

fold

fold

fold

fold

Princess

Bag

Cut out

Cut out

fold

fold

fold in

Stand

Cut out slot

Cut out slot.
Slot stand into here

Crown

Glue to other end of crown

23

Stitched and beaded

goodies

COOL Crafts!

Felt badges

Make a cute dog badge to attach to a jacket, bag, or hat. Once you've learned the technique you can make a range of designs, including a sheriff's badge, a monster, or a flower brooch (see pages 28–29).

1 Trace or photocopy the felt shapes (see page 79) onto paper and cut them out. Pin the paper shape to the felt and cut carefully around it using sharp scissors.

2 Sew a black bead on one side for the dog's eye.

3 Stitch round the edge of the bow using blanket stitch (see page 80). Then sew it to the dog's body.

Do not finish the sewing but leave a length of thread to attach it to the body.

4 Sew around the dog's body using blanket stitch, leaving a gap on its back. Use running stitch (see page 80) when you reach its chin. Stuff the filling into its head, legs, and body using a pencil.

5 Finish stitching the dog's back with blanket stitch. To fasten off the thread, stitch over twice in the same place and then make a long stitch on the back of the badge. Pull firmly and cut the end, which will disappear into the dog's back.

6 Sew the brooch pin securely to the back of the badge.

Wear me on a hat!

Felt flowers

Surprise someone with these bright and pretty flower badges.

1 Trace or photocopy the shapes (see page 79) onto paper. Layer 2 pieces of felt together if 2 are required. Pin each paper shape to the felt and carefully cut around it.

2 Place the 2 big purple flowers together and stitch in running stitch (see page 80) around the edges. Sew the 2 smaller purple flower shapes together so the petals overlap. Sew the 2 orange circles together, adding a tiny amount of stuffing before finishing off the stitching around the circle. Stitch the 3 parts of the flower together.

3 To make the blue flower, layer the 2 pieces of blue felt together and stitch around the edges in running stitch. Join the red centre using running stitch, adding a little stuffing. Sew a brooch pin to the back of each badge.

Sheriff's badge

Keep law and order going with this cool sheriff's badge.

1 Trace or photocopy the shapes (see page 79) onto paper. Layer 2 pieces of felt together if 2 are required. Pin each paper shape to the felt and carefully cut around it.

2 Sew the small orange star to the light yellow circle, adding a bead to each point of the star and one in the middle. Use blanket stitch (see page 80) to attach the circle to the front piece of the large star.

3 Attach a brooch pin to the back piece of the badge. Sew the 2 large stars together using blanket stitch, adding in the beads to the points of the star as you stitch.

Friendly monster

This felt badge is a brilliant buddy that can be worn on a jacket.

1 Trace the shapes (see page 79) onto paper. Layer 2 pieces of felt together if 2 are required. Pin each paper shape to the felt and carefully cut around each one. Sew the spots onto the front of the monster's body and front arms. Sew in its teeth with 2 little stitches (the stitches give it a nose).

2 Blanket stitch the arms together and then the feet. Embroider lines for toes using back stitch. Sew the beads to the white eyeballs and then use blanket stitch to sew the eyes onto the head. Sew the front of the head to the body using blanket stitch.

3 Use blanket stitch to sew the front and back of the body together, sewing on the head, arms, and feet as you go. Stuff the body before completing and stitching. Add a brooch pin to the back.

Cute puppy

This lovely little puppy badge can be worn on a collar or rucksack.

1 Trace the shapes (see page 79). Layer 2 pieces of felt together if 2 are required. Pin each paper shape to the felt and carefully cut around it.

2 Make the dog's ears using a front, a back, and an inner pink piece for each one. Stitch the eyes to the patches, then use blanket stitch to attach the dog's patches and nose to the front of its face. Sew on the brooch pin to the back of the dog's head.

3 Use blanket stitch to sew the ears to the top of the head and to sew the front and back of the dog's head together. Insert the stuffing between the ears, before you close the gap with running stitch.

Woof, woof!

Felt bag

This bag is an ideal present. Everyone will be envious of it and you'll soon be getting orders to make more! Ask an adult to help you as there are a lot of steps.

You will need

tracing paper

pen

30cm x 30cm (12in x 12in) felt squares

pin cushion

scissors

needle   coloured thread

30cm (12in) ruler

black beads

ribbon   snap-on fastener

1 Trace the template designs on pages 76–77. Pin the paper to the felt and cut out the fox shapes (brown and white) and bag shapes (green). The bag uses the whole length of a 30cm (12in) square from edge to edge.

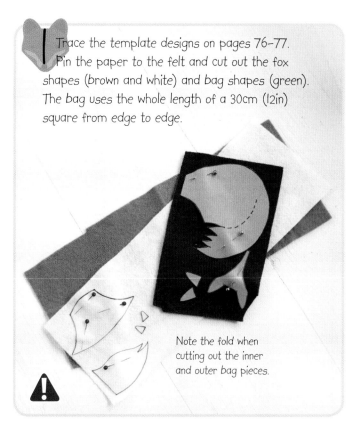

Note the fold when cutting out the inner and outer bag pieces.

2 Fold the bag piece (as shown on template) into the bag shape and position the fox's body and tail shape pieces to the bottom front of the bag. The brown part of the tail is placed over the felt of the tail tip to reveal the white tail fur. Pin in place. Unfold the bag. Use running stitch (see page 80) to sew the pieces on. Remove the pins.

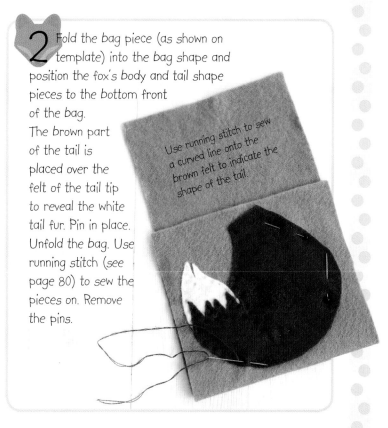

Use running stitch to sew a curved line onto the brown felt to indicate the shape of the tail.

3 Refold the bag inside out (so the fox is inside) and pin the sides of the bag together. Using a pen and ruler, draw a line along both 11cm (4¹/₃in) edge seams. Sew along the lines to join the edges together using backstitch (see page 80).

Turn the bag the right way out again and set aside.

4 Take the fox's face and use running stitch to sew on the little white parts of the ears. Sew the brown back pieces onto each ear. Pin in position then sew the brown face shape onto the centre of the white face shape.

Let the ears stick out above the head and leave a small space at the bottom for the nose bead. Sew on the eyes and nose beads using black thread.

5 Fold the bag again as shown on the template. Pin the head into a central position onto the front flap of the bag. The top of the head sits in line with the fold. Sew across the top of the head, from ear to ear, leaving the ears above the fold.

With pale thread, sew the white felt face onto the flap.

6 Turn the bag over. Cut a 168cm (66in) length of ribbon (for an adult's gift; less for a child), fold over 1cm (1/2in) of each end, and pin the ends to the top and back of the bag. This will stop the ribbon ends from fraying.

Sew the ribbon on with running stitch (see page 80). Remember to take care NOT to twist the ribbon!

7 Fold the white lining as shown on the template (see page 79). Blanket stitch (see page 80) up the sides leaving the top flap free, insert inside the green bag, and pin firmly in place. Then sew the inner (white) bag to the outer (green) bag by stitching around the edges of the flap and along the front opening.

Take a snap-on fastener and stitch one part to the white layer and the other to the front of the bag, on the fox's neck.

NOTE: Take care to stitch the fastener to the white layer only. If that's too tricky, stitch the fastener on BEFORE sewing the white bag to the green flap!

8 The finished bag is the perfect place for a mobile phone, keys or purse.

You can also make a felt bag (like the blue one below) out of thicker felt. This means you don't need to line it with another bag inside. Decorate it with speedy mini pom-poms (see opposite).

32

Speedy mini pom-poms!

All you need is a ball of wool and a fork to make these. Use them to decorate projects in this book.

1 String one end of the wool into the middle prong of the fork and use one hand hold it in place. Wrap the wool around the fork in layers (as shown).

2 Tie and knot a 15cm (6in) piece of wool as tightly as possible around the middle of the pom-pom.

Trim off the wool.

3 Cut the wool along the right side and left side of the fork. Then take it off the fork. Ta da! You have a mini pom-pom.

Get creative and design your own felt bag. Try making a bird or a cat.

Mouse in a tin

This adorable mouse in a tin is a bit tricky to make, so you'll need to ask an adult to help you. You'll love it so much it will be hard to give it away. It's a perfect present for all ages.

Turn him over and see he's already asleep.

A metal tin for mints is the perfect size bed for your mouse. Make a cosy sleeping bag out of felt.

You can make a toy bunny for him too!

1 Trace, photocopy, or draw felt shapes and cut them out. There is a template on page 78. You will need: body x 2, grey ears x 2, pink ears x 2, feet x 2, tail x 1, arms x 4.

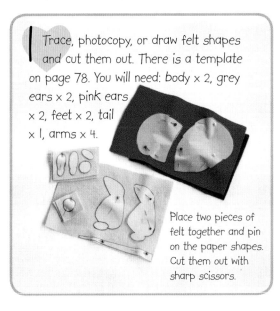

Place two pieces of felt together and pin on the paper shapes. Cut them out with sharp scissors.

2 Using running stitch (see page 80), first sew the ear pieces together one pink piece to one grey piece.

Fold in half (with the pink piece inside) and fasten with a stitch to hold the ear shape.

3 Sew the arm pieces together starting near the top of each arm down to the paws. Add a little stuffing, but not too much.

Do not finish the sewing, but leave a length of thread to attach it to the body.

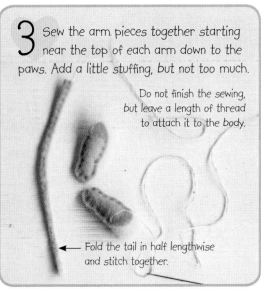

← Fold the tail in half lengthwise and stitch together.

4 Sew the black beaded eye on one side. Then embroider (or draw with a pen) the sleepy eye on other flipped front piece of mouse as shown.

Attach the arms to the body as you finish sewing them. Try to keep the stitches hidden inside.

Sew the extra foot pieces onto the mouse's feet.

5 Attach ears to the head by sewing them securely to the inside of the body pieces by stitching over twice. Stitch around the body, attach the tail and stitch it in as you go.

Add a stitch to hold the ears together.

Attach the nose bead.

Before you complete the sewing, stuff the body.

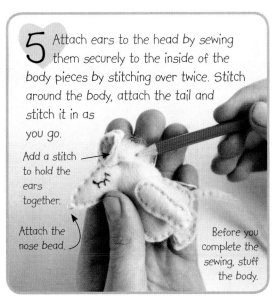

6 Cut out a dark and a light half leaf shape and a dark and a light full leaf shape. Blanket stitch (see page 80) the top of the two half leaf shapes together. Use running stitch for the veins.

7 Pin the darker sides of the leaf shapes together and blanket stitch around all the edges to complete the sleeping bag for your mouse. Put it in the tin.

Pom-pom scarf

This beautiful scarf is easy to create, but you'll need patience as you need to make 16 pom-poms! The scarf is incredibly warm so it makes a perfect Christmas gift.

TOP TIP
This warm and lovely winter scarf is the perfect present for mums, grannies, and aunts.

1 Use a pencil and compass to draw a circle 6cm (2½in) in diameter on card. Draw a circle inside about 2cm (¾in) across. Cut out the big circle and then cut a slit from the outside. Cut out the inner circle.

You will need two rings for each pom-pom so use this as a template to make another 31.

2 Thread 1m (3ft) length of three colours of wool onto a large needle. Place your card circles together with the slits at different angles. Pull the strands through the centre hole, round the outside and in again.

Wrap the strands all the way round as evenly as possible.

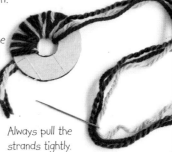

Always pull the strands tightly.

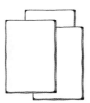

3 When the first strands have run out simply rethread the needle again and add more. Stop when the inner circle is filled right up and it's difficult to push the needle through. The strands should be wrapped evenly and plumply all around the outside.

4 Snip at the edge of the woolly circle down to the card edges then slip the scissor blades between the two circles to cut the threads all the way around.

5 Slip a length of wool between the two card circles, wrap it round the centre of the pom-pom twice, and tie it tightly. Gently prise the cards away from the wool so they leave the pom-pom.

Snip the ends off the stray strands to tidy the pom-pom.

Repeat steps 1–5 until you have 16 pom-poms.

6 Use a needle and strong thread to link the pom-poms. Thread through the core to halfway along the thread. Take the loose end, bring it round and knot it. Repeat.

7 Once all the pom-poms are made and joined together as in step 6, finish off the last one by knotting it between the last and second from last pom-pom cores.

Attach the key ring
to a loop on your
bag strap and
your beaded lizard
can come with
you everywhere.

Beaded lizard

These cute lizards make perfect gifts for everyone, including dads, uncles, and brothers. They can be used as key rings, or hung from belts, rucksacks, or even on curtains!

TOP TIP
Tape the metal ring to the table to hold the lizard in place and free up your hands.

1 Line up the ends of the cord. Take the middle point of the cord and push it through the key ring. Thread both ends of the cord through the loop and pull tight to close.

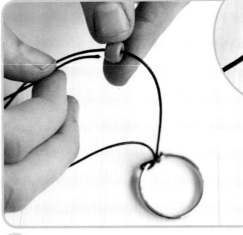

2 Take the ends of the cord and thread each of them through one of the green beads, one from the left and one from the right.

The two ends of the cord cross as they pass through the bead. Always do this and pull tight to keep the beads in place.

3 Pull the cord tight to move the tip of the nose into place. Thread 2 more green beads, together this time. Then a row of 3: yellow, green, yellow. The yellow beads make the eyes.

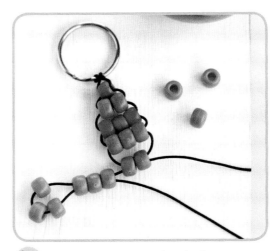

4 Add a row of 3 green beads, then a row of 2. Next thread 3 green and 3 blue beads onto one end of the cord and loop it back through the green beads to make an arm.

You will need

beads (2 x yellow, 18 x blue, and 43 x green)

Key ring

scissors

142cm (56in) black rat tail cord

Cross the ends of the cord over ready for the next step.

5 Repeat the process with the other end of the cord to make the other arm and then pull everything tight. You might need to adjust the beads a bit to straighten the arms.

6 Next, make the body. Using the crossover method described on page 39, thread 3 rows as follows: 2 green; then green, blue, green; then green, 2 blue, green.

NOTE: Always pull each row tight.

7 Pull everything tight, then finish the body by adding another row of green, 2 blue, green; then green, blue, green; and finally 2 green.

Ta da! Your lizard has a head, body and legs – all he needs is a tail.

8 Repeat what you did in steps 4 and 5 to make the lizard's 2 back legs.

Make the tail from single beads.

9 Cross the ends of the cord, then one by one thread 8 green beads onto the remaining cord to make the tail, crossing the cord through each bead and pulling tight.

10 Finally, tie a double knot in the string to keep everything together, and cut off any excess with a pair of scissors.

A lizard family

Try out different colours of beads to create lots of different lizards.

Make a brother or sister for your lizard by using 3 different colours of bead: one colour for the eyes; one for the feet and back; and one for the body, legs, and tail.

Or make a crazy stripy friend out of lots of different colours!

Moulded
and sculpted
treasures

Groovy
GIFTS!

You will need

265g (9½oz)
bicarbonate of soda

200ml (7fl oz)
water

65g (2oz)
corn flour

large saucepan

wooden spoon

large bowl

damp tea towel

rolling pin

cookie cutters

2 baking trays

baking parchment

wooden skewers

ring or other items to make indents

oven gloves

cooling rack

PVA glue

acrylic paints

paintbrushes

ribbons

Pretty pendants

These pretty pendants are a lovely gift on their own or as a set. You can be really creative with the indents you make on your pendant shapes and with the colours you paint them. They can be worn as a necklace or used as decorations.

When it looks like smooth mashed potatoes, remove from the heat.

1 Combine the water, bicarbonate of soda, and cornflour in a large saucepan and place on a medium heat. Stir continuously for a couple of minutes. It will soon begin to thicken.

2 Spoon the ball of dough into a large bowl and place a damp tea towel over the top until the mixture has completely cooled down.

Roll out the dough to 1cm (½in) thick.

Add more flour to the dough if it's too sticky.

3 Knead the dough on a smooth surface that's lightly dusted with cornflour. To avoid the dough cracking, knead it really well before rolling it out. Use cutters to make a range of shapes.

4 Ask an adult to preheat the oven to 110°C (225°C/Gas¼). Place the shapes on 2 trays, lined with baking parchment. Make a hole at the top of each shape with a skewer.

Try out various items to make indentations.

Double knot the ribbon so the pendant doesn't come off.

5 Make indentations on the surface of each shape. Bake for one hour, turning halfway through. When the shapes have completely cooled, cover them with a thin layer of PVA glue or clear nail polish.

Try making a smaller heart inside a larger one.

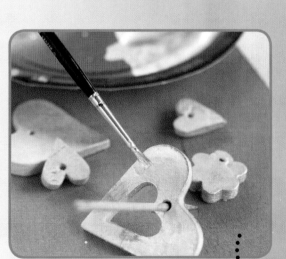

6 When the glue has dried, you can paint and decorate the shapes if you want to. Let the paint dry and then thread through ribbon to make a chain for each pendant.

Paint your pendant and add glittery nail polish.

PLEASE NOTE
Even though these pendants are made with items from your store cupboard, they are NOT edible.

45

Candle glass jars

These beautiful glass jars are a perfect gift for a birthday or a "get-well gift". You can make these at a party and then use them as "going home presents".

TOP TIP
If you don't have time to make pendants for the jars, try tying coloured ribbons around them.

You will need

tissue paper

hole punch

clear varnish

paintbrush

glass jar

assorted beads

strong wire

scissors

pretty pendant
(see pages 44–45)

tea light

1 First you need to cut out some flower shapes from tissue paper. The quickest way is to use a special hole punch to cut shapes from tissue paper. Use an array of colours.

2 Use clear varnish to stick the shapes onto the glass jar. Paint the jar first with a layer of clear varnish and then pick the delicate tissue shapes up with the same wet paintbrush.

3 Thread beads onto a length of strong wire. Make sure there are enough to go around the top of your glass jar. Attach to the top of the jar by twisting the ends of the wire together.

4 Make a pretty pendant to decorate your jar (see pages 44–45). Thread some wire through the pendant, string beads onto the wire, and attach it to the beads around the jar.

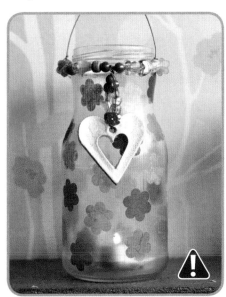

5 Make a wire handle by twisting a length of wire onto the wire that goes around the top of the jar. You can make the handle as long or as short as you like.

6 Put a tea light candle into the jar. Ask an adult to help by lighting the candle and placing it into the jar (with the jar on its side), then use a pencil to move the candle into position at the bottom of the jar.

TOP TIP
Present your flowers in a vase or jug. Add a ribbon to give your gift a splash of colour.

Plaster flowers

This plaster-dipped posy would be the perfect present for your mother, grandmother, or best friend. The plaster of Paris creates an everlasting bouquet that will stay beautiful all year round, adding a touch of spring to any room.

You will need

artificial flowers

strong glue

strong green wire cut to lengths of 20cm (8in)

eye goggles

large latex rubber gloves

large plastic cup

plastic spoon

8 tbsp plaster of Paris (CAREFULLY follow the instructions on the packet)

120ml (4fl oz) water

paintbrush

1 Remove the heads from the flowers and replace the stalks with wire. Secure the wire with strong glue.

Ensure each flower gets well coated.

2 Ask an adult to mix up the plaster to the consistency of thick glue. The adult can dip each flower into the plaster. Eye goggles and latex gloves should be worn when doing this.

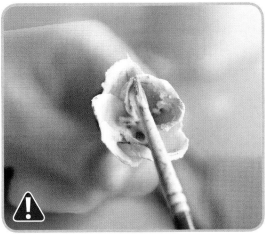

3 Ask an adult to use a paintbrush to cover any exposed parts of the flower with plaster. Eye goggles and latex gloves should be worn when doing this.

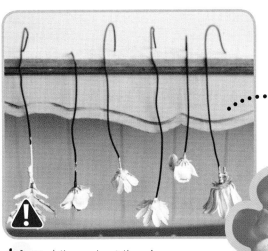

4 Curl the ends of the wire over to hang the flowers up to dry. Leave them for at least 1 hour, until dry, then curl the wire back and arrange your bouquet.

49

Make, bake, and create

treats

Divine
DISHES!

Coconut bites

These coconut bites are fun to make, and to eat!
They stay fresh for a couple of weeks so you can make
them up a few days before a birthday party and use
them as take-home swag bag presents.

TOP TIP
You don't have
to use cellophane
wrap. Try out other
types of packaging for
the coconut bites.

ALL WRAPPED UP

These coconut bites are super sweet, so make sure you only have a small portion at a time.

You will need

20cm (8in) square
cake tin

pastry brush

non-stick baking
parchment

mixing bowl

cookie cutter

olive oil

800g (1¾lb)
desiccated
coconut

1kg (2¼lb)
icing sugar

1kg (2¼lb)
condensed
milk

green food colouring
pink food colouring
blue food colouring
orange food colouring

1 Lightly oil a small but deep baking tin using a pastry brush and olive oil, and line it with non-stick baking parchment. We have used a square tin here, but any tin with straight sides will do.

2 In a mixing bowl, mix the desiccated coconut, icing sugar, and condensed milk. As the mixture becomes stiff you can use your hands. Divide the mixture in half.

3 Put half the mixture in the tin as the bottom layer. Smooth it over with your fingers.

4 Take the other half and divide it into 4 portions. Apply a couple of drops of food colouring to 1 portion and knead the colour in. Do the same to each of the 4 portions, using a different colour each time.

5 Form each coloured portion into a square the size of a quarter of the tin, then put them on top of the lower layer, to form the top layer. Leave in a cool place to set for 3 hours, or overnight.

6 Use a cookie cutter to create small round pieces. We have lined them up and wrapped them in cellophane wrap with ribbon ties, but you can choose your own style.

There's one for everyone.

Brownie jar

Make these delicious brownies as a gift for someone. Once they've tasted them they'll want to know how to make them. As an extra treat, give them a jar of the dry ingredients with the instructions on a gift tag (photocopy the tag template on page 76).

TOP TIP
Decorate the lid with homemade paper and tie a ribbon around the jar.

Use lots of shallow layers to make the jar look amazing.

Use a sieve to dust cocoa over the top of the brownies before you cut them.

Dry ingredients for the jar

100g (3½oz) chopped hazelnuts

½ tsp baking powder

15g (½oz) cocoa powder

300g (10oz) soft light brown sugar

125g (4½oz) plain flour, sieved

100g (3½oz) white chocolate, broken into pieces

Other ingredients and equipment

2 eggs

1 tsp vanilla extract

small bowl

large mixing bowl

oven gloves

sieve

wooden spoon

baking tin 20cm x 15cm (8in x 6in)

150g (5½oz) unsalted butter

saucepan

glass bowl

cooling rack

fork

90g (3oz) plain chocolate, broken into pieces

spatula

olive oil

non-stick baking parchment

pastry brush

1 Ask an adult to preheat the oven to 180°C (350°F/Gas 4). Lightly oil a baking tin using a pastry brush and olive oil, then line it with non-stick baking parchment.

2 Melt the butter and plain chocolate in a bowl over a saucepan of simmering water, stirring occasionally. Remove from the heat and allow to cool slightly.

3 In a small bowl, use a fork to whisk the eggs and add the vanilla.

4 Tip all the dry ingredients into a large mixing bowl. Pour the melted chocolate and butter into the mixture and stir in.

5 Add the eggs and vanilla mixture, then use a rubber spatula to mix everything thoroughly. There should be no flour visible.

6 Pour the mixture into the tin and smooth over with a spatula. Ask an adult to bake the brownies for 25 minutes. Place on a cooling rack until cooled. Cut into 20 squares in the tin.

Rocket cookies

These glittery and colourful cookies melt in your mouth.
They're an exciting treat to give to a friend or as party
gifts to take home. Present them in a star-covered
cardboard box or bag that
you can make yourself.

TOP TIP
Be treat-wise.
These cookies taste
as good as they
look! Limit yourself
to 1 cookie.

Add a bit of
sparkly space
dust to your
cookies.

To decorate

500g (1lb 2oz)
icing sugar, sifted

water

red food
colouring

blue food
colouring

silver sugar
balls

silver edible
glitter

1 Ask an adult to preheat the oven to 180°C (350°F/Gas 4). Line the trays with baking parchment. In a large bowl, rub the butter into the flour until it looks like breadcrumbs.

2 Whisk the egg in a separate bowl and then add it to the flour. Add the sugar and golden syrup and combine well until it all forms a soft dough. Chill for 10 minutes.

3 Roll out the dough to 5mm (¼in) on a floured surface and cut out shapes using the rocket and star cookie cutters. Place the shapes on the trays. Re-roll the dough and cut out more shapes until all the dough is used (it makes 15–20 cookies).

4 Insert a coffee stirrer into the back of each cookie. Ask an adult to bake the cookies for 15 minutes, or until golden, then place on cooling racks.

5 To make the piping icing for the cookie outlines, place the sifted icing sugar into a large bowl. Add water a little at a time and mix until it forms a smooth consistency with soft peaks. Spoon a portion into a piping bag.

6 Gently squeeze the bag to pipe an icing outline on each cookie. Allow it to set. Transfer two-thirds of the remaining piping icing into a large bowl and water it down so it's runny. Use a spoon to "flood" the cookies with the runny icing.

Divide the leftover piping icing into 2 portions. Colour 1 red and 1 blue. Pipe it onto the cookies. Decorate with silver balls and edible glitter.

Hearty rolls

These tasty bread rolls are a healthy treat to give to someone, and are delicious with butter and jam. Try presenting them in a homemade gift box.

They look appealing wrapped in tissue paper

58

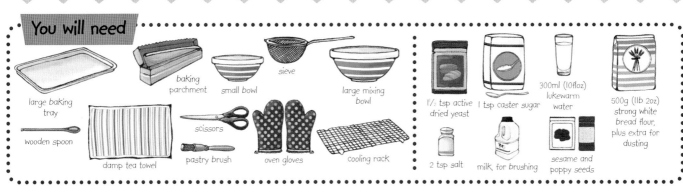

You will need

large baking tray

wooden spoon

baking parchment

small bowl

sieve

large mixing bowl

damp tea towel

pastry brush

scissors

oven gloves

cooling rack

1½ tsp active dried yeast

1 tsp caster sugar

300ml (10floz) lukewarm water

500g (1lb 2oz) strong white bread flour, plus extra for dusting

2 tsp salt

milk, for brushing

sesame and poppy seeds

1 Line a large baking tray with baking parchment. Place the yeast, sugar, and ¼ of the water in a small bowl. Stir well and leave in a warm place for 10 minutes, until frothy.

2 Sift the flour and salt into a large bowl. Make a well in the centre and pour in the yeast mixture and remaining water. Stir with a wooden spoon to form a dough.

3 Knead the dough on a lightly floured surface for 10 minutes. Place back in the bowl, cover with a damp tea towel and leave in a warm place for 1 hour or until doubled in size.

4 "Knock back" the dough, by lightly punching it. Then knead it on a floured surface. Shape the dough into 6–8 heart shapes. Make a small cut at the top of each roll. Place on a baking tray. Cover with a damp tea towel and leave to rise in a warm place for 30 minutes.

5 Ask an adult to preheat the oven to 220°C (425°F/ Gas 7). Brush the tops of the rolls with milk and sprinkle with either type of seed, or just scatter flour on top.

6 Ask an adult to place the baking tray in the centre of the oven. Bake the rolls for 30 minutes or until golden. Tap the base of the roll – it should sound hollow. Place on a cooling rack to completely cool.

Flowerpot cakes

These tasty treats are perfect for a Mother's Day gift or for a birthday party. They almost look too good to eat! You will need to begin by making the cookie dough to use for the flowers and leaves from the recipe on pages 56–57.

recipe on pages 56–57

You will need

8 paper coffee cups

6 paper espresso cups

8 muffin paper cases

6 cupcake paper cases

scissors

large mixing bowl

wooden spoon

large baking tray

cooling rack

14 wooden coffee stirrers

150g (5½oz) unsalted butter, softened

150g (5½oz) caster sugar

150g (5½oz) self-raising flour

3 medium eggs, whisked

½ tsp vanilla extract

6 tbsp milk

50g (1¾oz) chocolate, cut into chunks

100g (3½oz) cocoa powder

1 Ask an adult to preheat the oven to 180°C (350°F/Gas 4). Put the cupcake cases into the espresso cups and the muffin cases into the coffee cups. Cut the cups down if need be.

2 Place the butter, sugar, self-raising flour, eggs, vanilla extract, milk, chocolate chunks, and cocoa powder in a bowl and beat with a wooden spoon until well mixed.

3 Spoon a portion of the mixture into each muffin/cupcake case and put them on a baking tray. Ask an adult to put the trays in the oven for you and bake for 20–25 minutes.

4 When the cakes feel springy to the touch, ask an adult to remove them from the oven and let them completely cool on a cooling rack. Decorate the tops with grated chocolate.

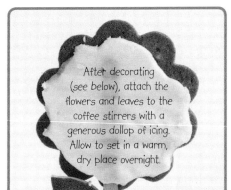

50g (1³/₄oz) grated chocolate

400g (14oz) icing sugar

water

green and orange food colourings

icing piping bag

After decorating (*see below*), attach the flowers and leaves to the coffee stirrers with a generous dollop of icing. Allow to set in a warm, dry place overnight.

5 Make 8 large flower-shaped cookies and 6 small ones, and 22 leaf-shaped cookies. Ice them following the method on page 57, leaving a space in the centre of each flower, and putting aside some of the icing to make orange centres for the flowers, green leaves and white detail on the leaves. When set, attach them to the coffee stirrers.

Use 2 leaves with large flowers and 1 with small ones.

6 When the icing has completely set, insert a flower into each cake; large flowers in the coffee cups and small flowers in the espresso cups.

Cover paper cups with pretty paper or buy patterned cups.

Be treat-wise. These flowerpot cakes are really sweet. Eat the cake first and save the cookie for the next day.

Pop art cupcakes

2 × 12-bun tins

20 paper cases   2 mixing bowls

wooden spoon

metal spoon

Knife

cooling rack

rolling pin

round cookie cutters

150g (5½oz) unsalted butter, softened

150g (5½oz) caster sugar   150g (5½oz) self-raising flour

3 medium eggs, whisked

a range of food colourings

500g (1lb 2oz) ready rolled icing   ½ tsp vanilla extract

sprinkle of icing sugar, for dusting

This recipe makes 20 cupcakes so you can give them all away as one gift on a tray, or package them up into a few gift boxes for different people. You can ice lettering onto each cupcake to form a message such as, "I love you mum".

1 Put 20 paper cases into the bun tins. Ask an adult to preheat the oven to 180°C (350°F/Gas 4).

2 Place the butter, sugar, self-raising flour, eggs, and vanilla extract in a bowl and beat with a wooden spoon until pale and creamy.

3 Divide between the paper cases. Ask an adult to bake the cupcakes for 15 minutes until golden and just firm. Cool in the tin for 5 minutes, then transfer to a cooling rack to cool.

4 Trim any pointed tops to make a flat surface on each cupcake. Make sure you aim the knife towards the work surface and away from your body.

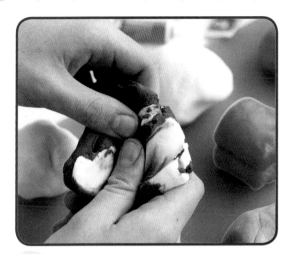

TOP TIP
Take a photo of your cakes before you give them away. They're like a work of art so you want to keep a record of them.

5 Divide ready-to-roll icing into 15 portions and add a small drop of food colouring in each portion to create an array of colours. Use your fingers to knead in the colour. Wash your hands in between making each colour.

6 Lightly dust your work surface with icing sugar. Roll out the icing portions into thin layers about 5mm (¼in) thick. Use 3 different sizes of cookie cutters to cut out the circles. Carefully layer them onto each cupcake.

Gingerbread

These delicious biscuits are a lovely treat to give to someone at Christmas. Wrap them up in tissue paper, in a gift bag, or make a special gift box.

TOP TIP
If you have time, you can make your own piping icing (see page 57 for instructions).

You can use a cut down juice carton for a gift box. Paint and decorate it to make it look like a gingerbread house.

You will need

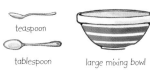

large baking tray x 2

baking parchment

teaspoon

tablespoon

large mixing bowl

350g (12oz) plain flour

2 tsp ground ginger

1 tsp bicarbonate of soda

125g (4½oz) butter, diced

150g (5½oz) soft dark brown sugar

wooden spoon

rolling pin

cookie cutters

wooden skewers

oven gloves

cooling rack

4 tbsp golden syrup

1 medium egg, beaten

shop-bought icing, to decorate

sugar decorations of your choice

1 Ask an adult to preheat the oven to 180°C (350°F/Gas 4). Line the baking trays with baking parchment. Place the flour, ginger, and bicarbonate of soda in a large bowl. Stir the ingredients until they are mixed well.

2 Rub the butter into the mixture using your fingertips. Continue rubbing in the butter until the mixture resembles fine breadcrumbs. Stir in the sugar.

3 Stir in the golden syrup and egg, until the mixture starts to come together in a dough. Tip the dough mixture onto a lightly floured surface and knead it until smooth.

4 Use a rolling pin to roll out the dough on a lightly floured surface to a thickness of 5mm (¼in), then using your cutters, cut out the shapes. Re-roll the leftover dough and cut out more biscuits. Place on the baking trays.

5 Use a skewer to make a little hole in each cookie (to thread with ribbon later). Ask an adult to bake the biscuits for 10 minutes or until golden. Allow them to cool on the cooling rack. Finish off with the icing and decorations.

6 If you like, thread each gingerbread biscuit with ribbon once the icing has set. They're perfect Christmas decorations – if they don't get eaten straight away!

Tea party

As an extra-special present, invite a friend or relative over for an afternoon tea. Lay out your feast and decorate the table before your guest arrives. They will absolutely love these delicious scones.

TOP TIP
You can make individual stands for the scones out of paper cups and strong card.

You will need

large mixing bowl

round-bladed knife

wooden spoon

rolling pin

star-shaped cookie cutter

sieve

pastry brush

oven gloves

large baking tray

cooling rack

50g (1³/₄oz) butter, diced

250g (9oz) self-raising flour

1 tsp baking powder

50g (2oz) caster sugar

150ml (5fl oz) milk

pinch of salt

beaten egg or milk for brushing

To serve

jam

whipped cream

1 Ask an adult to preheat the oven to 220°C (425°F/Gas 7). Lightly grease the baking tray with some butter. Sift the flour, baking powder, and salt into a large mixing bowl. Add the butter.

2 Using your fingertips, rub the butter and flour mixture together until it resembles fine breadcrumbs. Stir in the sugar with a wooden spoon and mix together thoroughly.

3 Stir in the milk with a round-bladed knife until the mixture forms a soft dough and comes together in a ball. Gently knead the dough on a floured surface to remove any cracks.

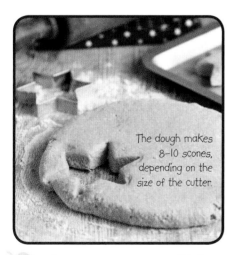

The dough makes 8-10 scones, depending on the size of the cutter.

4 Roll out the dough to 2cm (³/₄in) thickness, then using a star-shaped cookie cutter, cut into individual stars. Gather up any trimmings, re-roll them and cut out more scones.

5 Place the scones on a baking tray, spacing them a little apart. Using a pastry brush, cover the tops with the egg or milk. Ask an adult to cook them for 10-12 minutes, or until golden brown.

6 Transfer the scones to a cooling rack. When cool, cut them in half, spread with whipped cream and jam, and replace their lids.

Beautifully wrapped up

projects

COOL PAPER!

TOP TIP
Use a variety of
patterned or
coloured paper
to make the
butterflies.

Present bags

Once you've made a gift you need to give it away in something. Present bags made from cereal boxes are perfect as they're big and sturdy. Get creative and try out lots of designs. Here's one to get you started.

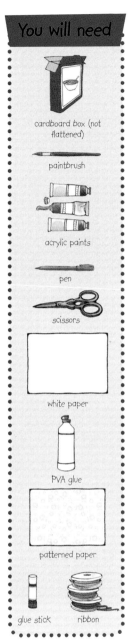

1 Paint the outside of a cereal box with light blue acrylic paint. You can also paint the top of the inside section if you want.

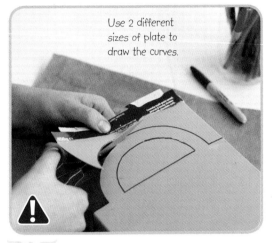

Use 2 different sizes of plate to draw the curves.

2 When the paint has dried, use a pen to draw out handles at the top of the box. Cut out the sections you have marked up.

3 Cut out the cloud shapes from white paper. Glue them on the front and back of the box.

4 Draw butterfly shapes on the back of patterned paper. Cut them out and fold the wings up slightly. With a glue stick, put glue on the back of each butterfly (but not the wings), then stick them on the bag.

Tie it up with a ribbon.

Special post

The next time you want to give somebody a letter or a card, make it extra special by using a homemade envelope. The person you give it to will love how personal it is.

Make sure the heart is even on both sides.

1 Take a sheet of hand-printed paper and fold it in half over the middle. Neatly draw a heart shape on the plain side, as shown above.

2 Cut the heart out along the lines you drew. Fold the 2 sides into the middle, leaving just a little bit of space so they don't touch.

3 Using your fingers to keep the sides tucked in, fold the bottom up over the middle towards the pointed top. Use a glue stick to glue the insides of the folds down.

Glue 2 pieces of paper together in step 1 to give your envelope a lining.

4 Smooth down all the edges. Once you've put something inside, just fold the pointed top into the middle and tuck it in to seal it.

Make your own writing paper too.

Cut out a heart from pink paper and write a message on it. Fold it in half to fit inside your envelope.

Use a range of stamps (which you can buy from most stationers) to make pretty hand-printed paper.

You will need

foam stamps

ink pads

sheets of A3
coloured paper

glitter gel pens

scissors

ribbon

TOP TIP
To get a more faded
effect, use a scrap
piece of paper to blot
your stamp before
using it.

Wrap up a present
to see the full effect
of your amazing
homemade paper.

It's a wrap!

Make your own beautiful handmade wrapping paper
using foam stamps and coloured inks, available from
most stationers. Add your own decorations and impress
everyone who receives a present from you.

1 Buy a few designs that you like and test your
stamps on a sheet of paper to get a feel for
how to use them and how much ink they need.

2 Choose the stamp design, paper colour,
and ink that you want to use and spread
out the paper on a flat surface.

3 Get stamping! Carefully stamp your design
all over the paper, making sure you avoid
smudging the ink with your hand as you move
across the paper.

4 Use gold and silver gel glitter pens to add
extra sparkle to your paper. You can fill in
detail on the stamped patterns, or draw new
decoration in the spaces between.

Tag it!

Use your stampers to make terrific tags! Cut around a stamped design and glue it onto a shop-bought paper tag.

Let a little bird carry your message!

Glue small paper butterflies (wings folded upwards) onto a tag.

Cut out and fold 5 paper hearts. Glue them down.

Stamp out a flower design, then make the stalk and leaves from scrap paper, or hand draw them.

Make up a batch of wrapping paper, wrap it with ribbon, and store it away, ready for the next birthday or special occasion that comes up.

75

Templates

A handful of projects require templates in order for you to make the craft.

BIRD CAGE

FIND ME pp8-9

Use this bird, unless you want to design your own.

photocopy the bird and cut out

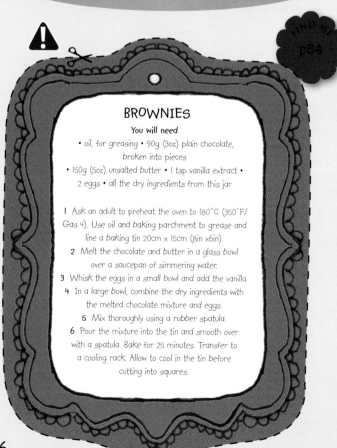

FIND ME p54

BROWNIES

You will need

• oil, for greasing • 90g (3oz) plain chocolate, broken into pieces
• 150g (5oz) unsalted butter • 1 tsp vanilla extract •
2 eggs • all the dry ingredients from this jar

1 Ask an adult to preheat the oven to 180°C (350°F/ Gas 4). Use oil and baking parchment to grease and line a baking tin 20cm x 15cm (8in x6in).
2 Melt the chocolate and butter in a glass bowl over a saucepan of simmering water.
3 Whisk the eggs in a small bowl and add the vanilla.
4 In a large bowl, combine the dry ingredients with the melted chocolate mixture and eggs.
5 Mix thoroughly using a rubber spatula.
6 Pour the mixture into the tin and smooth over with a spatula. Bake for 25 minutes. Transfer to a cooling rack. Allow to cool in the tin before cutting into squares.

⚠ FELT BAG

FIND ME pp30-34

Photocopy the templates for the felt bag and cut out the pieces to pin to the felt as a guide.

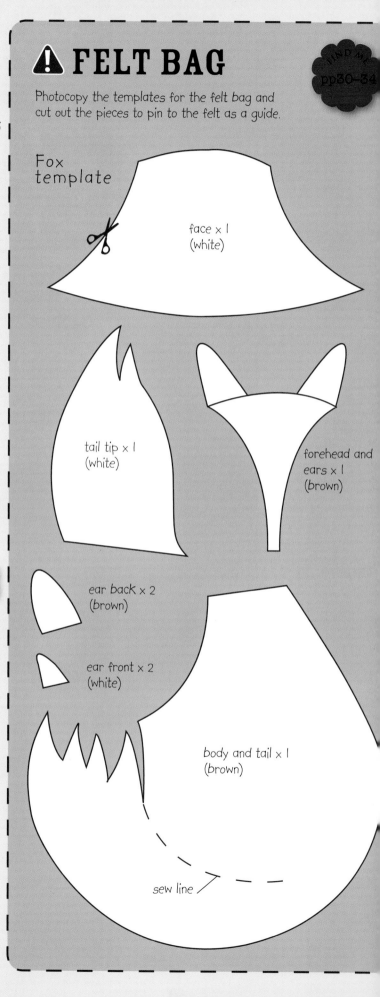

Fox template

face x 1 (white)

tail tip x 1 (white)

forehead and ears x 1 (brown)

ear back x 2 (brown)

ear front x 2 (white)

body and tail x 1 (brown)

sew line

Outer pocket of bag (green) – total length of felt 30cm (12in)

cut

mark felt along line for stitching

fold felt
over here,
so this
section is
double

outer top flap
of bag (trim
to fit when
fox's head is
stitched on)

mark felt along line for stitching

cut

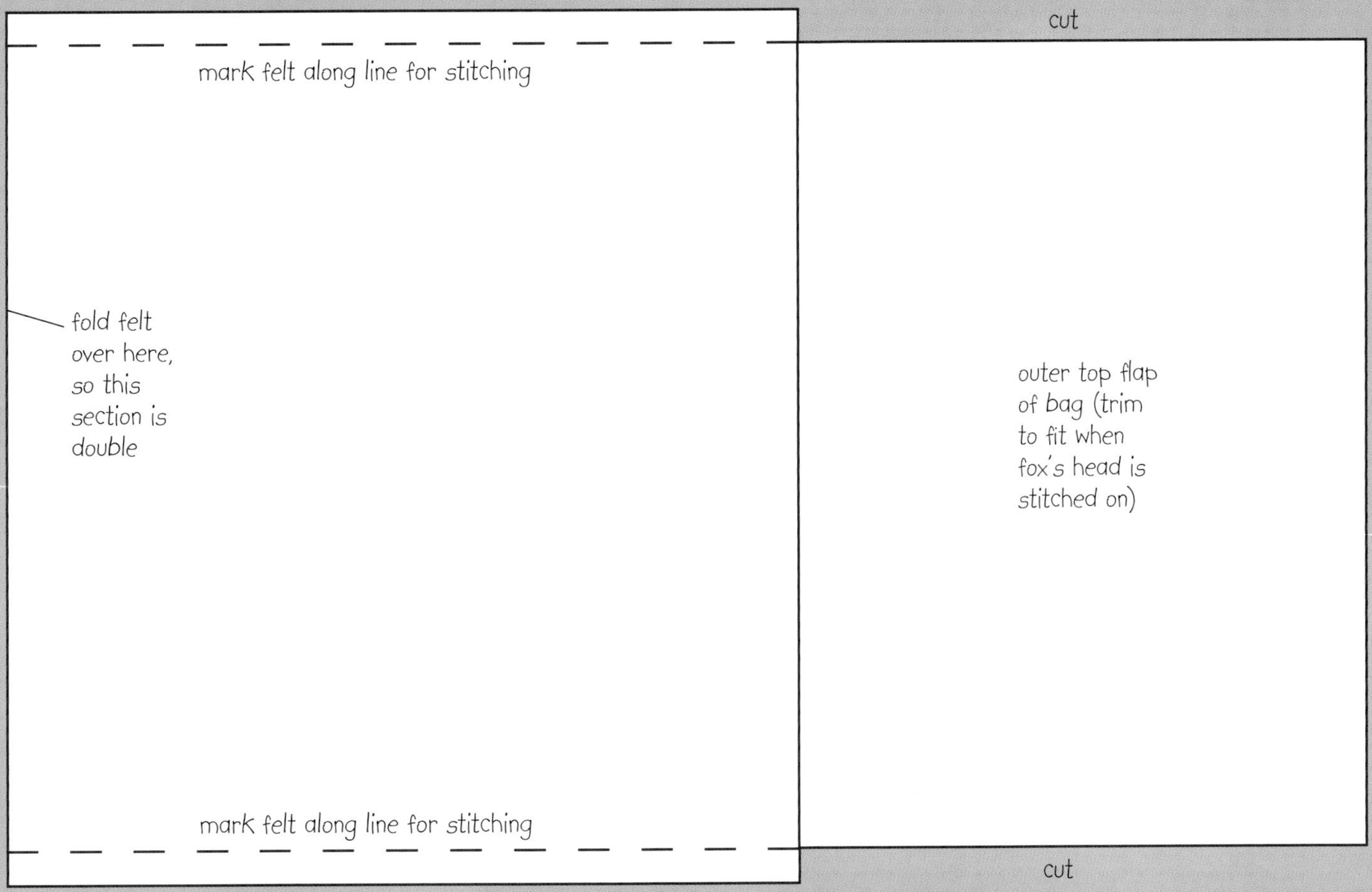

Inner pocket of bag (white) – total length of felt 30cm (12in)

fold felt
over here,
so this
section is
double

inner top
flap of bag
(trim to fit
when fox's
head is
stitched on)

position of
fastener

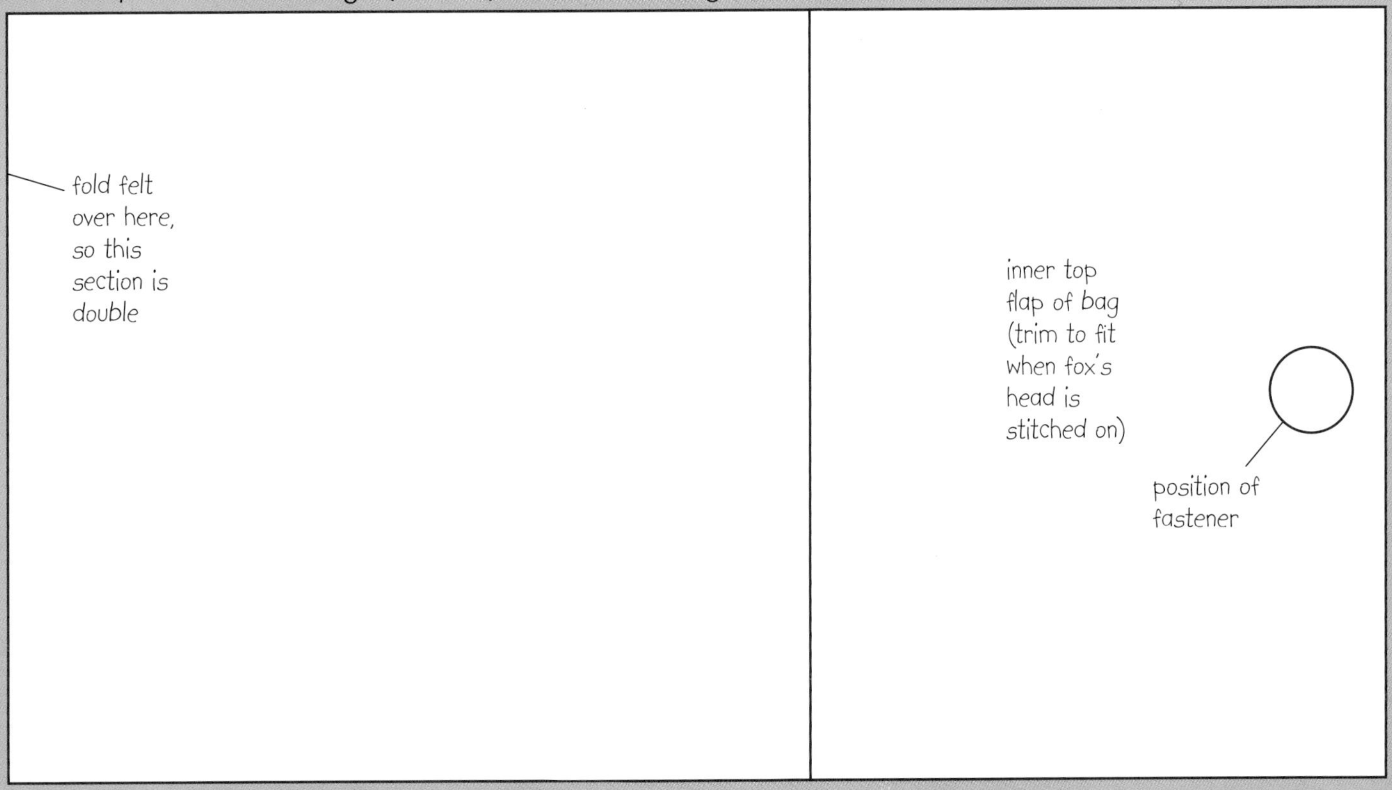

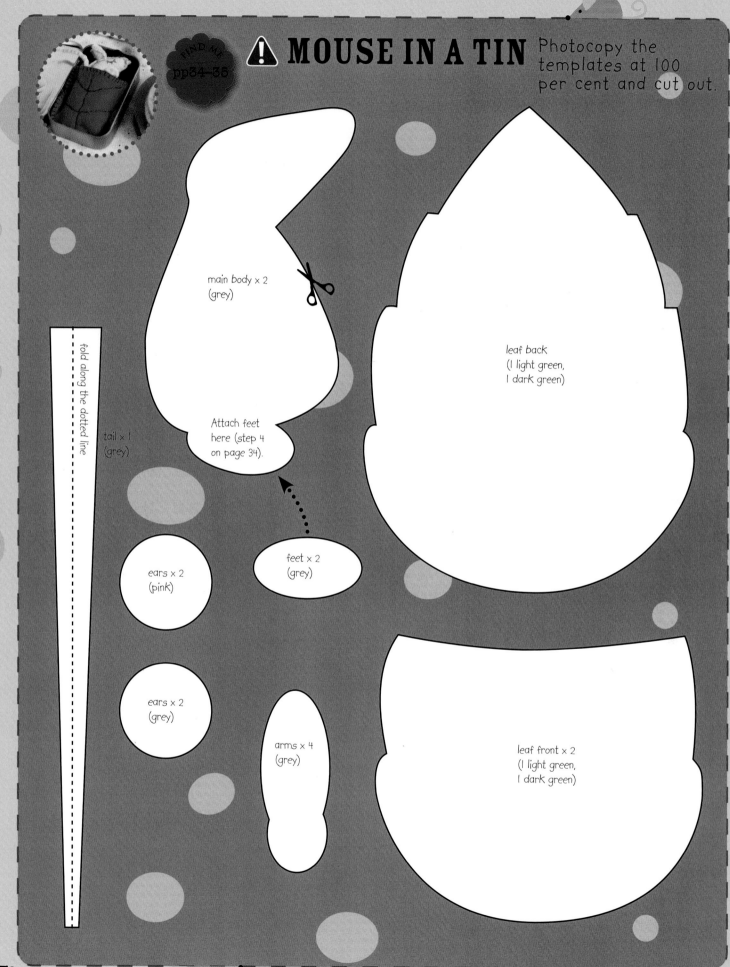

FIND ME
pp34–35

⚠ **MOUSE IN A TIN** Photocopy the templates at 100 per cent and cut out.

main body x 2
(grey)

leaf back
(1 light green,
1 dark green)

fold along the dotted line

tail x 1
(grey)

Attach feet
here (step 4
on page 34).

ears x 2
(pink)

feet x 2
(grey)

ears x 2
(grey)

arms x 4
(grey)

leaf front x 2
(1 light green,
1 dark green)

⚠ FELT BADGES

Photocopy these templates to a size that you are comfortable making.

You will need

tracing paper • pen
• felt squares • pins
• fabric scissors • needle
• embroidery threads • beads
• polyester stuffing • brooch pins

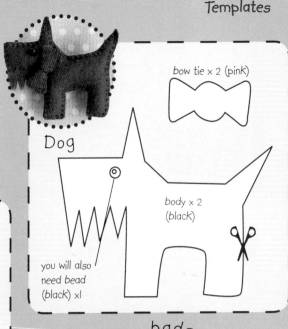

Dog

bow tie x 2 (pink)

body x 2 (black)

you will also need bead (black) x1

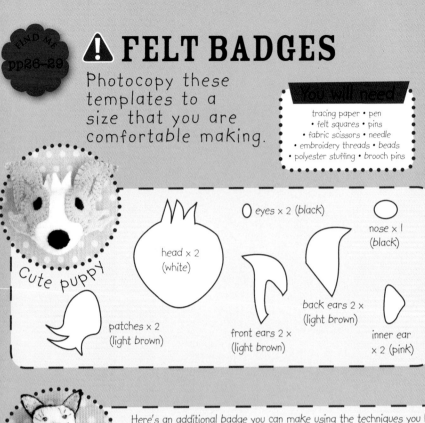

Cute puppy

head x 2 (white)

eyes x 2 (black)

nose x 1 (black)

back ears 2 x (light brown)

front ears 2 x (light brown)

inner ear x 2 (pink)

patches x 2 (light brown)

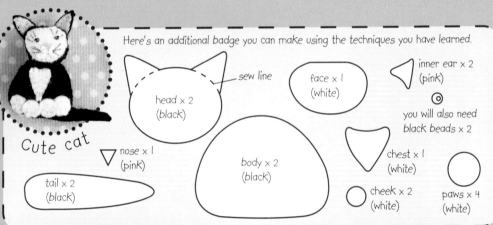

Cute cat

Here's an additional badge you can make using the techniques you have learned.

head x 2 (black)

sew line

face x 1 (white)

inner ear x 2 (pink)

you will also need black beads x 2

chest x 1 (white)

body x 2 (black)

nose x 1 (pink)

tail x 2 (black)

cheek x 2 (white)

paws x 4 (white)

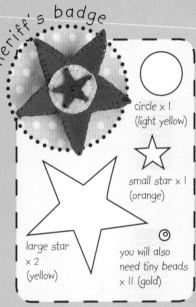

Sheriff's badge

circle x 1 (light yellow)

small star x 1 (orange)

large star x 2 (yellow)

you will also need tiny beads x 11 (gold)

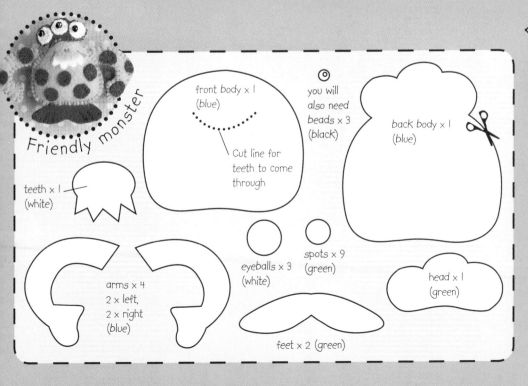

Friendly monster

front body x 1 (blue)

you will also need beads x 3 (black)

back body x 1 (blue)

Cut line for teeth to come through

teeth x 1 (white)

arms x 4
2 x left,
2 x right
(blue)

eyeballs x 3 (white)

spots x 9 (green)

head x 1 (green)

feet x 2 (green)

Felt flowers

centre x 2 (orange)

small flower x 2 (purple)

big flower x 2 (purple)

centre x 1 (red)

flower x 2 (blue)

Index

How to start and finish

Begin stitching with a knot at the end of the thread. To end a row of stitches, make a tiny stitch, but do not pull it tight. Bring the thread back up through the loop and pull tight. Do this once more in the same spot, then cut the thread.

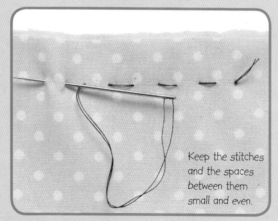

Keep the stitches and the spaces between them small and even.

Running stitch

This is a very versatile stitch used for seams, sewing fabric together, and for gathering.

Make the stitch then bring the needle back to the place where the last stitch is finished.

Bring the needle out ready to begin the next stitch.

View from reverse

Backstitch

This is the strongest stitch. It makes a continuous line of stitches so it is best for sewing two pieces of fabric securely, like the sides of a bag.

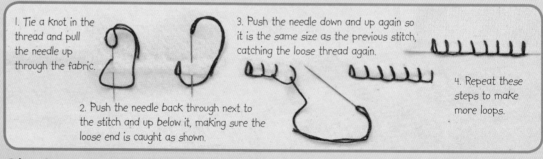

1. Tie a knot in the thread and pull the needle up through the fabric.

2. Push the needle back through next to the stitch and up below it, making sure the loose end is caught as shown.

3. Push the needle down and up again so it is the same size as the previous stitch, catching the loose thread again.

4. Repeat these steps to make more loops.

Blanket stitch

This stitch is good for making neat, decorative edges and for sewing one piece of fabric to another.